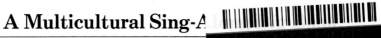

IT'S PINK, I THINK

Kathleen Beal

1. Do you like my T - shirt? Yes, I do.___ It's pink, I think. I like your T - shirt.

2. Do you like my hat? Yes, I do.___ It's green and pink, I think. I like your hat.

3. Do you like my belt? Yes, I do.___ It's white, and green, and pink, I think. I like your belt.

Music by Dwight Beal

A Publication of the World Language Division

Project Director: Elinor Chamas
Editorial Development: Elly Schottman
Production/Manufacturing: James W. Gibbons
Design/Art Direction: Joanna Fabris
Illustrator: Bari Weissman

ISBN 0-201-52206-3
13 14 15 16 17 18 19 20-WR-0100999897

✲ Addison-Wesley Publishing Company

Reading, Massachusetts • Menlo Park, California • New York • Don Mills, Ontario
Wokingham, England • Amsterdam • Bonn • Sydney • Singapore • Tokyo • Madrid • San Juan

Do you like my T-shirt?

Yes, I do.

It's pink,
I think.
I like your T-shirt.

Do you like my hat?

Yes, I do.

It's green,
and pink,
I think.
I like your hat.

Do you like my belt?

Yes, I do.

It's white,
and green,
and pink,
I think.
I like your belt.

Do you like my jacket?

Yes, I do.

It's black,
and white,
and green,
and pink,
I think.
I like your jacket.

Do you like my dress?

Yes, I do.

It's yellow,
and black,
and white,
and green,
and pink,
I think.
I like your dress.

Do you like my pants?

Yes, I do.

They're orange,
and yellow,
and black,
and white,
and green,
and pink,
I think.
I like your pants.

Do you like my sneakers?

Yes, I do.

They're red,
and orange,
and yellow,
and black,
and white,
and green,
and pink,
I think.
I like your sneakers.

Do you like my socks?

Yes, I do.

They're blue,
and red,
and orange,
and yellow,
and black,
and white,
and green,
and pink,
I think.
I like your socks.

Do you like our clothes?

Yes, we do.

They're blue,
and red,
and orange,
and yellow,
and black,
and white,
and green,
and pink,
I think.
We like your clothes.